If I Die Before You Wake

poems by

Steven Lewis

Finishing Line Press
Georgetown, Kentucky

If I Die Before You Wake

For Clay, Devin, Bella, Connor, Rory, Maddie, Schuyler, Jack, Charlee, Eleanor, Cade, Bridger, Emma, Hattie, Maggie, Delilah, and ??? (... when they awake)

Copyright © 2017 by Steven Lewis
ISBN 978-1-63534-205-5 First Edition
All rights reserved under International and Pan-American Copyright Conventions.
No part of this book may be reproduced in any manner whatsoever without written permission from the publisher, except in the case of brief quotations embodied in critical articles and reviews.

ACKNOWLEDGMENTS

Grateful acknowledgment is made to the editors of the following publications, where some of the pieces in this collection first appeared.
Spirituality & Health: "If I Die Before You Wake," and "What Do You Want to Be" (originally published as a prose piece titled "Fleeting")
Millrock Writers: "A Month on a Barrier Island: Day 6"
Paterson Literary Review: "Floaters," "Loon Memory" (original title "Why Not")
Talking Writing: "Tell Them" (original title, "In My 70th Year")

Publisher: Leah Maines

Editor: Christen Kincaid

Cover Art: Steven Lewis

Author Photo: : Edward McCann (www.Read650.com)

Cover Design: Elizabeth Maines McCleavy

Printed in the USA on acid-free paper.
Order online: www.finishinglinepress.com
 also available on amazon.com

Author inquiries and mail orders:
Finishing Line Press
P. O. Box 1626
Georgetown, Kentucky 40324
U. S. A.

Table of Contents

Introduction: If I Die Before You Wake

FROM THE BEGINNING OF TERROR

What Do You Want to Be 1
A Month on a Barrier Island: Day 6 3
Loon Memory 4
Wandering the Desert 5
This Campfire 6
But You 7
If I Spring a Leak 8
You Got to Know Where You Live 9
Tell Them 11
Now Tell Me 13

THE END OF TERROR

Floaters 14
Shoulder to Shoulder 15
Anatomy of a Black Snake Murder 16
Down in the Animal Marrow 18
"Only the Moonlight Showing" 19
Sailing to Rodanthe 20
Tomorrows 21
Such Uneasy Joy 22
What You Know 23
Windfall 26
Cradling Despair With Ellen Bass 28

EPILOGUE

Transfer at Croton-Harmon 30

To suspect your own mortality is to know the beginning of terror, to learn irrefutably that you are mortal is to know the end of terror.

Frank Herbert

INTRODUCTION: IF I DIE BEFORE YOU WAKE

A MEDITATION ON WORDS

At nine, curled up under a Roy Rogers blanket, the cold breath of death blew across my dark dormered bedroom. I shivered and instantly knew this one simple truth: no matter what I would do, no matter whom I would please, no matter how good I could be, I was doomed to die. That knowledge not only made my lower lip tremble in fear but raised chronic decades-long goose bumps on my arms.

That night my father sat on my bed and smiled and said that I wouldn't die for a long long long time. "A hundred years," he said. And when that didn't produce the magic relief he intended, he told me that I wouldn't die at all—ever.

Even at nine, I knew that wasn't the truth. I knew I was going to die. Sooner or later. So I wasn't comforted. More troubling, I knew that my parents would not always tell me the truth, they would just try to make things all better. Even things that could never be all better.

Even so, I was comforted.

Now fast forward on that frigid tailwind through adolescence, college, marriage and kids … to a harder than soft landing in the reflective present, which includes a small tribe of 16 grandchildren who call me Chief: I am now 70 and, practically all illusions left behind at one unsanctified cathedral or another, I can feel that cold wind breathing down the back of my neck. Such is life.

In looking back on the dark nights and light years that followed that unfateful fateful evening when I was nine, I can see how I did the same thing my father did … offering "innocent" affirmations intended to protect my tender-hearted children from the harsh truths about life on this cold planet. Seven times over I repeated the one that begins with "You can be anything you want to be," as well as the one that ends with "…and they lived happily ever after."

Not "… and then they died." Mea culpa.

That said, I'm not donning a hair shirt over my repeated failures to speak truth to my children. In recent years, as I've watched my children tell similar lies to their children, I've come to understand that it is the parents' job to encourage their children, no matter the realities, with the hope that they might grow up to be confident and fearless adults.

The elders of the tribe, though, are beholden to a different call.

INTRODUCTION: IF I DIE BEFORE YOU WAKE

And with the horizon growing closer every day, I am more interested in the sanctity of my grandchildren's souls than the soothing of their fears. I am moved to tell them truth. Truth that is audacious, stunning, revelatory ... even frightening. Truth that might actually set them free from fear.

So I awaken these days and come to the keyboard with the singular intention to write poems and stories that will someday be read by my grandchildren (and hopefully many others) with some confidence that, even if I might surprise or shock or appall, I will not lie.

And if I die before they "wake"—and, frankly, I don't think anyone truly awakens before the age of twenty-five—here is the one truth to begin it all:

Although some of us may be lucky enough to be healthy and safe and cherished and loved by family and friends, in the universe outside our homes, beyond our tribes, across tree lines and down subway lines, no one is beloved enough to be escape the fate of being human. No one is special. Each of us is, as T.S. Eliot wrote, "... whirled by the cold wind / That blows before and after time."

That is the core truth. The fearful poetry of life.

But there is some solace in that cold wind: once we accept that singularly lonely truth, we can finally give up trying to control the universe and learn humility in our bones, forgiveness in our bellies, kindness in our hearts, love in our souls.

FROM THE BEGINNING OF TERROR

WHAT DO YOU WANT TO BE
    For Eleanor Marie Lewis

Five-year-old Eleanor and I are swinging in the hammock
on the upper deck of a beach cottage
on Hatteras Island when she takes her thumb
from her mouth and asks, "How old are you, Chiefie?"

"Sixty-six" I say. "That's old!" she says
and slides the thumb back in her mouth.
I nod, feeling all of sixty-six
and maybe more, pressing my cheek

onto her sun bleached hair, brown pelicans
soaring in formation just over the crest
of waves beyond the hurricane-flattened dunes.
So I change the subject: the grandparent

fallback: "What do you want to be
when you grow up?" Eleanor curls up
in the hollow of my shoulder and doesn't speak.
Five? Ten? Fifteen? minutes later, the two us

swinging in the warm humid breeze
on criss-crossed ropes hung from 8X8 posts,
when she removes her thumb and says,
"I want to be thirty, Chiefie."

"Thirty?" I smile, charmed beyond understanding.
"Thirty," she says and the thumb slides
back between her lips. "Why thirty?" I ask,
but she doesn't answer, she turns over again

and snuggles into the other hollow. And when I lean
over to see what's happening out in the hazy distance
at the end of the pier, she takes out the thumb:
"I don't want to be little when you die," she says.

FROM THE BEGINNING OF TERROR

In the breathless silence that follows her
pronouncement, waves crashing, willets skittering
at the edge of the surf, I don't ask
this beautiful golden child, who doesn't yet know

addition or subtraction, how she arrived
at the transcendent formula to calculate the age
when she won't feel so small and vulnerable
anymore, when losing me won't hurt so much.

So I ask if she's hungry, and when she nods
we slip down off the hammock, clamber
down the rickety steps and into the empty beach cottage
where she stands on a chair while we make

cheese and tomato sandwiches on white bread
with big slathers of mayonnaise. And because her parents
are on the beach with the rest of our big tribe,
I pour us two glasses of root beer.

We eat then, the two of us all alone in the little cottage.

FROM THE BEGINNING OF TERROR

A MONTH ON A BARRIER ISLAND: DAY 6

An unplanned 15 minute nap
under the afternoon sun, half in, half out of a dream of waking,

my baking eyes open
to empty beach chairs all around, a surfboard out in front of my feet,

a water jug, a towel covered with sand, white
clouds drifting in front of the sun, dark shadows in the light green water,

shallow to the chest out to the shoal
where I spot my wife, the love of my whole adult life,

and rise to join her,
wading into the foam, diving under the crashing

wave, shark-like, belly inches from the bottom, feet humping
fingers reaching reaching until

I explode out of the sea with a gasp and grasp a thigh
expecting some girlish shriek, but

but find only an accommodating smile, having seen me all
these years angle up from some beach chair,

dive under one and then another green wave, just
a silly boy under this tanned and scarred skin.

FROM THE BEGINNING OF TERROR

LOON MEMORY

When you come upon a loon,
Good Friday
on this Hatteras beach,

molting, stranded,
hunkered down
in sand, low tide,

unable to fly
even the ten yards
to surf, you

wrap a towel
around the quivering body
and pick her up

in your bare arms, where she coos
and coos as your wife
drives you, you and your loon,

over to Pamlico Sound
where you place her in a bed
of reeds at water's edge,

watch her lunge herself
into the shallows, warm
and brackish, paddling

off beyond sight,
beyond loon memory,
her weight still in your arms

FROM THE BEGINNING OF TERROR

WANDERING THE DESERT

Our baby girl, skinny doll legs
up in a sling at the Hospital for Joint Diseases,

her mother leaning over
a metal crib, bare breast falling into her open mouth,

texts me a picture 23 years later
from New Mexico, her current *love-of-my-life*

in front of a tent, their dog, ass to the camera phone
mountains in the background.

Back home the love-of-my-life leans
over my shoulder, stares silently into the tiny screen,

each of us wandering
alone in this desert, parched, wondering

where we've been, how we got here,
where she's going, does she have enough to drink.

FROM THE BEGINNING OF TERROR

THIS CAMPFIRE

Been sitting around
this campfire
for millions of years,

cold mouth of the cave
behind, dark forest
beyond the fiery circle:

coyotes, bears, foxes, fisher cats
padding along the tree
line, turkey vultures up in branches,

hawks on ledges, my tribe,
shouldered in left and right,
my warrior friends

hunched across the flickering
flames, wind blowing
smoke in my face,

eyes burning, head
turning like a barred owl,
so when I look up again

one man has disappeared
into darkness. Another still
sits there but has left

the circle without a word.

FROM THE BEGINNING OF TERROR

BUT YOU
    For Patricia

The snow starts at the Virginia line, powdery flakes
drifting across picked cotton fields,
a jagged white line in the furrows
where soybeans bloomed green last summer.

By the Chesapeake it looks like a Lake Erie blizzard, cold
blossoms like tiny white birds
blowing down from the heavens
and swooping up just before they hit the windshield.

In a Delaware whiteout, on Route 1, now following nothing but
red tail lights and dark tracks,
dark tracks, red lights, I pledge
against this cold unseasoned myopia to stop for the night

in Jersey, where slipping, skidding over the peak of the Memorial
Bridge, hellish lights ahead,
I lose all sense and break my fearful pledge, steel
belted rubber turning and turning and turning in deep slush

rolling through this emptied darkness, far far inland from the cold
and thankless ocean,
I am heading home, I am leaning forward, I am
a hood ornament hawk, a black hawk crossing the last state line,

fingers now talons gripping
a frozen bent branch, beak in the wind,
all the way home all the way home and all the way home
all the snowy way home for all that snowy way home until I am all

the way home, I think of nothing else, I think of nothing else,
nothing else, nothing else, nothing else
no one else, no one else, no one,
no one, no one but

you.

FROM THE BEGINNING OF TERROR

IF I SPRING A LEAK

My father gone ten years, I glance
at the vast blue oceans, above and below,
my skin, brown and thick as a rubber raft, lungs
inhaling exhaling salt air, I was floating

through this watery life for a decade
before my holy friend Neil pulled the plug
on that ark in July, then my righteous sextant Jim
abandoned his agony in November.

So when my sainted Lake Michigan Captain fell
overboard in March, I couldn't breathe,
a jagged hole in my hull, trapped air rushing
into air, arms shriveling into prayer

these bleeding wet palms pressed to my chest.

FROM THE BEGINNING OF TERROR

YOU GOT TO KNOW WHERE YOU LIVE

Tony, who grew up in Plaquemines Parish,
is taking us by boat to his camp
down a long No Wake canal in the swamps
meandering like a gator around Venice, Louisiana.

Tony, who grew up in Plaquemines Parish,
Cajun drawl, sweet as redfish
flesh, cuts the engine and lets the current
carry us to a dock where he ties up

in front of a small cottage, wooden swing
on the front porch, new metal roof
glinting in the quiet sunlight. Tony,
born and bred in Plaquemines Parish

tells us how quiet this camp
gets at night, no buzzing wires, no phones,
no flushing toilets, no generators, just billions
of bugs, the flap of wings, slap

of a mullet flipping out of the water, gator
slipping onto the bank. Inside the cottage,
wood panels from his grandpa's barn,
paintings by nieces and nephews on the sloped

ceiling, an endless landscape of bending reeds
off the back deck, I am leaning on the rail,
inhaling blue sky when Tony points
to the loft, and we follow up the ladder,

a massive bed for him and his wife,
who spends the week up in Covington, dark
granules of gritty something spread
on the plywood floor: "Snake

FROM THE BEGINNING OF TERROR

Away," Tony explains before I ask.
And before I ask, "You got to know
where you live," he says and turns
to climb back down the ladder

out the open door to the dock, a great blue gliding by,
cottonmouths and water moccasins, somewhere,
everywhere silent and unseen, an osprey
way up in a dead cypress, watching it all

as I watch Tony Fricke, of Plaquemines Parish,
Louisiana, cast out a line, smooth as silk,
reels in a flopping catfish. Then another, flip-
flopping on the deck. "Four fee-lays," he says.

FROM THE BEGINNING OF TERROR

TELL THEM: 04.30.2015

Wandering now barefoot across this meadow, scorching
midday sun, Queen Anne's Lace, purple
loosestrife scratching my ankles, a familiar voice

rising through rustling grasses saying *You,
you walk toward the silver maple,
beyond which a stone well appears*

in a swale of land where urgent thirst
overcomes good sense and I swing a leg
over the smooth hard edge, slowly,

slowly, toehold by grasping toehold, lowering
myself, clawed fingertips slipping
in then out of the damp spaces between round stones

until my I am standing at the edge of a stream,
kneeling in moss, cold water dripping
through curled fingers before it reaches

my parched tongue, shafts of sunlight,
glistening bubbles now lighting the way
around a bend to a mossy hut, a door

swinging open, a man I barely recognize
in a white robe, a sad smile,
opening his arms, his arms around

my shoulders, his warm moist breath against my ear,
that oddly familiar scratchy voice whispering *Time
to cut the crap, Steve. You don't know*

*anything about anything, God or karma or Hemingway
or hydrofracking or the military-industrial complex
or the benefits of Coenzyme Q10 or bok choy, I mean Jesus, man,*

FROM THE BEGINNING OF TERROR

he says, holding me, breathless now, my sweaty
hands pushing back against the thick love
handles beneath his cool as silk robe, *You,*

*you, you damn fool, you who
have written a million two million words
and still do not know*

*what makes a good sentence
 good or what makes words
wordless as the flight of birds.* Shit

*man, you don't even know why
you are here with me,* that bony hand
grabbing my elbow, rushing me

back along the stream,
an angry father, pointing me
back up the damp well

to the sunny meadow,
to the yellow clapboard house
that appears in the shade,

*or why I am taking you
to the ones who wait for you
but not you,*

*who love you
beyond all reason. Beyond
any human understanding. Go*

*ahead, man! Walk up those steps.
Open the damn door.
Tell them all.*

FROM THE BEGINNING OF TERROR

NOW TELL ME

Put away
that cherished
mother of pearl
butter knife, the toast, the margarine,
the sweet sing-along songs
your mother sang
to you when your
tummy was upset.

Here's an anise seed. Take it
for the acid in your stomach,
if you have gas, a runny nose,
if your urine stream slows down,
if you need to increase your appetite,
your sex drive. Take it. It won't work.
Then you'll tell me, finally,
about that grisly ache in your belly.

THE END OF TERROR

FLOATERS

I wish it were other-
wise, and those good men would just

show up at night, marauding through
my dreams with bloody scabbards, or else

be sitting at the foot of my bed
in flannel shirts, smiling uncles, nodding as if all is

well. But they only come in broad
daylight, blurred faces, floaters drifting across my glistening eyes,

and no, don't be silly, they don't threaten
or weep, don't even put a manly arm around my shoulders.

No. They just remind me of something or
other, then move into a dark corner, out of sight,

just like they did in life
another disembodied name no one in the world

knows but me in this lonely male sequence: Steve
Vermilye, Bruce Schenker.

Jim Hillestad, Jim Hazard, Neil Selinger, Marty Rosenblum,
Jon Kotcher, Ken Kogan, Dennis Niswander

   … meteors without tails, drifting
right to left, left to right, into some abyss I don't have a name for

THE END OF TERROR

SHOULDER TO SHOULDER
For Steve Kowit (1938-2015)

I knew you before I knew who you were,
those soulful poems in *The Sun,*
that cottony voice speaking to me
as if we were shoulder to shoulder

at some dive bar somewhere, maybe
Milwaukee, maybe Newark, rusted
container ships in the distance, I don't know,
I didn't know you, didn't know you

lived on the other coast,
didn't realize you were my old pal's
cousin, never glanced over
at the stool by my elbow,

just some other guy
pulling on a beer
talking like we were
what? friends? drinking buddies?

SDS vets? two angry strangers
finding communion in unfairness,
ancient suffering, some common
sadness just outside the heavy door,

a silence to be shared, the grand hope
of language, this unspoken love
making a poem warm brandy flowing
down a parched throat, cold beer

chasing it into darkness
where you have gone, my friend,
where I will never find you, the blinding
sun when we walk outside.

THE END OF TERROR

ANATOMY OF A BLACK SNAKE MURDER

This murder begins with squawking
wrens, then a pair of bluebirds scolding,
fluttering, circling, swooping, screeching, some
thing moving in the weeds around the garden,
below the birdhouses up on posts
eggs or fledglings inside, we don't know,
dead or alive, we don't know. We
don't know. What we do know
is that some animal wants to eat their babies
in those dark wooden boxes, tiny
birds folded in delicate shells
or open-mouthed and squeaking,

maybe a raccoon, a weasel, a snake,
oh, it is a snake, a big black hose
curled up in the bush below the wren
box; and when I poke it with a stick
it slides through the wire fence
into the vegetable garden, tail now twitching
in the straw bed as I follow it, poke it
again and again, then jump on the raised beds
when it comes after me, tongue darting, blood
pounding in my ears as if my heart might
explode before the tail disappears

in a rotting railroad tie. Now everything is silent,
everything waiting, as it always is,
as it was before the swooping
and scolding began,
but I am still shaken, shaking
over the kale, willing the damned creature
to move along to the chipmunks in the barn,
the mice in the shed, but I know what I know,
and so I already know what I'm going to do,
what I must do, even if I don't want to do it,

THE END OF TERROR

even if it appalls me, even if it condemns me
to my own righteous damnation of another
who would commit the same fearful act,
and I grab a hoe leaning on the fence, poke
and poke the hungry creature out of its hole, shadow it

onto the lawn and wait 'til it pauses, then
raise both hands and bring the blade down
again and again and again on the thick black body until
its jaws open wide and its head

is separated from body, thumping artery
in my neck, blood on the rusted metal,
I slide the misused hoe under the lifeless being,
now hanging like a thick rope
over the long wooden handle
and run over to the tree line, fling
it into the woods for some coyote padding
silently along the edge of the woods,
a red tailed hawk swooping
in from the cliffs while I

hose off the blade, speckles
of blood disappearing in the grassy earth,
then place the tool back where it had been
leaning on the garden post, and return
to my own wooden house for wine, for dinner,
then sleep, unsettled dreams of wandering
through empty bedrooms, waking the next morning
to walk barefoot to the tree line.

Head gone. Black hose gone.
A solitary bluebird fledging without sound,
without warning.

THE END OF TERROR

DOWN IN THE ANIMAL MARROW

After all the prayers, the holy incantations,
every body knows down in the animal
marrow that God cannot be

a Jew or a Christian or a Muslim
or anyone's savior who appears
at the edge of whatever cliff you find yourself,

dangling by your fingertips. And so you know
right there in the bowels that Love
is not all there is, is not a silk parachute

you discover in a cloud while falling
through the ether after you can no longer cling
to that cliff. And in plummeting down

to that rocky canyon you learn
in a shrieking instant, that health is fleeting,
that there are no platitudes to catch your fall

even as you lay bleeding, broken and bereft
flat on your back, fatefully aware now
that safety is never found

in numbers, in money, in poetry, in sweat
lodges, in sanctuaries, in war, in peace,
in prosperity, in sweet innocent babies:

Nothing can stop the ache borne into your soul.
All you can do, if you can pick yourself up,
is pick yourself up, brush off the dust,

spit away the blood,
look around at the vast dumb universe,
and go hunt for your next meal.

THE END OF TERROR

"ONLY THE MOONLIGHT SHOWING"
For Martin Jack Rosenblum

At sleep I imagine my old friend heard a squall
moving west across Lake Michigan
then

dreamt
of towels on a deck rippling
off the railing on some warm Gulf island,

driving rain splattering against the murmuring window. He
turns on his side, dreams his hand resting
on

thin
cotton covering her soft hip
and she reaches behind, long fingers, her breath in his mouth

THE END OF TERROR

SAILING TO RODANTHE

She glances at the white bandage on his forearm, listens to his sheepish
one-word explanation, then says, "It's going to look like a scar." It

is a three-inch tattoo of Hatteras Island, a narrow barrier reef, a scythe-
like hook right where you'd find the famous lighthouse. Like a scar. He

has to withstand all the smirking that follows him around town. They
assume it is just another laughable item in the inventory of aging

male attempts to recapture some virility. And he knows he'd be
an old fool, a tattered coat upon a stick, to say they're wrong. So

he doesn't say that the tattoo is also a talisman, a token, a cave drawing,
more about where he is going than where he's been. He doesn't say that

with this graven image on the inside wall of my arm,
after I run out of breath through the cool autumns and the darkening

winters to follow, all it will take is a quick turn of the wrist
and I'll find my way back to this island,

the arc of azure sky and green water,
shifting shoals beneath my slowly treading feet

THE END OF TERROR

TOMORROWS

Tomorrow, Monday, I'll be
the coyote I've always been,
loping through these woods,

howling, gnawing on the mess
the gods make of nature. But on
Tuesday I'll be the painted bunting

my wife yearns to see but never finds;
and Wednesday, the blockheaded dog who
follows her everywhere she goes, at least

until Thursday when I'll slip into
my elephant skin, trumpeting, lumbering
through the vast Savannas of Fridays and Saturdays

until I reach Sunday and become
a cold clear watering hole, thousands of
droplets being sprayed into his dry mouth.

THE END OF TERROR

SUCH UNEASY JOY

These days, long past knowing the planet
suffers the disease of being human, all that
suffering, hunger, pain, regret, I still

drive cross this river at dusk, tilled fields,
waving grasses, that gorgeous ridge
across the entire span of a windshield,

the blue blue blue sky above it all,
a red tailed hawk, some turkey vultures,
Springtown Road following the river,

another dead squirrel near the Humpo,
three baby deer on Cragswood Road,
and knowing that my days on this earth

are numbered, I can't stop myself
from wondering how I might
contain this beauty, these moments of grace,

without the ache of what I know today
coming down the long gravel drive,
glancing at the rise where the dogs are buried,

trees down from the tornado a few years past,
and yet I step out into the bright sunshine,
yellow house, green grass, bears in the woods,

birds in the trees, my love in the house,
such uneasy joy, one more perfect
moment in this harrowing free fall from the cliffs.

THE END OF TERROR

WHAT YOU KNOW
    For Nancy Colkin Tsoubris (1970-2016)

I.

After standing beside yourself
in the back of the church, watching

the anguished faces of her sister,
her husband, her children(!) passing by,

you see her bereft mother, her forsaken father
and your shadow self disappears,

your body fills with their ache. You know
even if you don't know.

2.

In the parking lot you meet
a former student, Alan Lazarus,

and although you are not
a man who finds meaning

in signs, you wonder
if this is not a sign,

so when you breathe in
you hear a rale in your chest.

3.

Turning out of the church parking lot
onto Cedar Valley Road, you are already angry,

as you are often angry when the covenant
is broken, when a child dies

THE END OF TERROR

before a parent, when all the empty
platitudes, the comfortless shibboleths burn

your ears with a pain you don't know
even when you know it all too well.

4.

On Route 9, Pink Floyd's ghastly scream
shatters your angry silence and The Wall speaks

to you as if it is 1988, the year Nancy Colkin
walked so full of hope into your class.

And although you are not a man
who finds meaning in signs, you wonder

if this is not a sign to pull off the pavement
and smash into someone's precious stone wall.

5.

On Route 299, a Warren Haynes'
guitar riff rattles your chest

so you crank and crank
the volume until you fear

the thumping speakers
will explode with everything

you know you know
you don't know.

THE END OF TERROR

6.

Now nearing home, at the fork
of Mountain Rest and Springtown Roads,

you know what you know, and so you know
that although you are not a man

who finds meaning in signs,
there ahead is a road sign that lets you know,

this way or that, it makes no difference,
sooner or later, all roads lead to the home you know.

THE END OF TERROR

WINDFALL

Wind at my back, I'm pedaling
like a boy racing away from school

down Route 12, Hatteras blue sky, sea oats leaning
toward the lighthouse 25 miles away,

grateful to be 70, alive, kids, grandkids,
48 years with the same woman, I am

singing the refrain from Son Volt's "Windfall,"
over and over, the only words of the song I know,

*both feet on the floor, two hands on the wheel
let the wind take your troubles away ...*

But when I make the turn a few miles down
at the Salvo graveyard, the heat now rising

under my hat, the first beads of sweat sliding
down my forehead, sagging eyes stinging,

thighs burning, wheels wobbling
through patches of blown sand along the shoulder

I squeeze the handlebars, lean into wind,
and so suddenly I'm grousing like some old man

muttering about ignorant bigots,
deplorable self-serving money makers,

jackasses who beat women,
who abuse boys and girls,

kill wild animals for sport,
send children off to war, hate

THE END OF TERROR

brown-skinned people, hate Jews
hate Muslims, hate everyone not their own

and then call it Freedom, call it
Manifest Destiny, call it God, following madmen

who laugh at their stupid loyalty
then sneer at grumblers like me, pedaling

and pedaling into wind, both feet on the floor,
two hands on the wheel

all the way back to a small beach cottage
at the edge of the surf, grateful

to be alive, to be 70,
kids, grandkids, 48 years, never enough

THE END OF TERROR

Cradling Despair with Ellen Bass: 04:30:2016

Today I see how it begins with those packaged jokes
about 40 being "over the hill,"

and then there's that clichéd witticism
of 50 being middle-aged (*bwah* ha ha!)

which leads right into the rib
tickler about 60 being the new 50.

Well, the jig is up at 70. No
more jokes. No more snarky asides

for willing audiences desperately
willing to believe they will

live forever, despite those irksome
reminders from the reptile brain,

those increasingly cranky joints,
obituary pages in black and white,

friends, parents, worse, children
dropping off the edge of sentences

into senseless condolences for which
there are no punchlines, no gags,

no miracles, nothing left but the grinning,
like chimpanzees, clapping

like toddlers, everyone applauding
your long marriage, your long life,

as if dumb chance has no role
in surviving anything. At 70

THE END OF TERROR

you finally know better.
You know you didn't do anything

to get here. You know God
did not choose you over another.

You know the days
spread out in front of you

will be bitter and sweet,
kind and cruel, frigid loneliness,

warmhearted love, much too soon over
and sometimes not soon enough,

small brush fires heading
toward some cool mountain stream.

EPILOGUE

Transfer at Croton Harmon

Along long empty beaches
in Esterillos Este, Manuel Antonio.
Playa Dominical, riding Patti Smith's
M Train through Wegener's theory of
the continental drift, I drift off
into some tidal pool when this notion
rolls in over the rocks:

Shakespeare was a bully;
Virginia Woolf was a spoiled brat;
Allen Ginsberg wet his pants;
Joan of Arc was a tattle tale; Mother
Theresa was a mean girl; Einstein, Nietzsche,
Sophocles, Eleanor Roosevelt, Marie Curie,
Jane Austen disappointed their parents every day.

The list goes on. Feral children grow
into civilized adults. The continents drift
farther apart. Some disembodied conductor
from my past says passengers must change
trains at Croton-Harmon; I look
out the streaked window, see the M Train
passing by and suddenly know

it never stops until you've had
enough, until you have become
a child again, until you have bent
your knees, standing on one forsaken
land mass, then leaping above
the blue widening ocean,
landing someplace else.

STEVEN LEWIS is a former Mentor at SUNY-Empire State College, current member of the Sarah Lawrence College Writing Institute faculty, and longtime freelancer. His work has been published widely, from the notable to the beyond obscure, including *The New York Times, The Washington Post, Christian Science Monitor, LA Times, Ploughshares, Narratively, Spirituality & Health* and a biblically long list of parenting publications (7 kids, 16 grandkids). He is a Contributing Writer at *Talking Writing* and Literary Ombudsman for *650: Where Writers Read*. His books include *Zen and the Art of Fatherhood, Fear and Loathing of Boca Raton*, a novel, *Take This*, and a generational sequel, *Loving Violet*, to be published by Codhill Press in summer 2017.

Steve writes, "During much of the 1960s I was writing self-indulgent poetry in Madison, Wisconsin—mostly to meet girls—but somewhere along the way the poet James Hazard gave me a flashlight to navigate my way through the self-reflective shadows and into what I now understand is the illuminating voice. It is the most valuable gizmo in the battered tool chest I carry daily up to my writing space in the Shawangunk Mountains and into workshops in New York's Hudson Valley and the windy beaches of Hatteras Island, NC." www.stevelewiswriter.com

www.ingramcontent.com/pod-product-compliance
Lightning Source LLC
LaVergne TN
LVHW041601070426
835507LV00011B/1238